THE BEECHER TRIAL:

A

REVIEW OF THE EVIDENCE.

REPRINTED FROM THE NEW YORK TIMES OF JULY 3, 1875.

WITH SOME

REVISIONS AND ADDITIONS.

NEW YORK:

1875.

THE BEECHER TRIAL.

THE jury in the Beecher case, after deliberating eight days, came into court with the announcement that they were unable to agree upon a verdict. The conflicting views which prevailed among twelve men who had the advantage of hearing all the witnesses examined and cross-examined have been shared by the public at large. But as we pass beyond the reach of those potent local influences which necessarily pressed heavily on the jury—for a man was under trial who in Brooklyn had been treated almost as a god—the divisions of opinion are found to be more strongly marked. There are many who will always hold that the plaintiff's case was fully proved. A second class will continue to believe Mr. Beecher innocent; while a third will consider that the Scotch verdict of "not proven" would have been the only just conclusion to reach. And there are comparatively few who will not in their hearts be compelled to acknowledge that Mr. Beecher's management of his private friendships and affairs has been entirely unworthy of his name, position, and sacred calling.

The evidence in the case has been so voluminous that we should ill discharge our duty if, before taking leave of the trial, we neglected to review it with some little care. The case naturally divides itself into four parts. There is, first, the charge itself, and the train of circumstances surrounding it. This must be considered, secondly, in connection with Mr. Beecher's acknowledged relations towards all the parties. Thirdly, it will be necessary to recall the manner in which Mr. Beecher met the charge. Lastly, we shall have to examine the answers to the charge. We shall endeavor to present a connected narrative of the case observing strictly the order of events; and in doing this we propose to confine ourselves exclusively to the documents or evidence produced on the trial, and to disregard all outside narratives or statements. The sole exception to this rule which we shall make is in reference to the "Marietta letter," the authenticity of which is not disputed, although it was not admissible as evidence on the trial.

I.—*THE ORIGIN OF THE CHARGE.*

The defense reposed in a great degree upon the theory that the charge of adultery was never brought against Mr. Beecher throughout the negotiations and correspondence which preceded the trial. In order to maintain this, it is necessary to assume not only that all the witnesses for the plaintiff committed perjury, but that Mr. Beecher was ignorant of what went on in the internal government of his own church. For Tilton swears, and Mr. and Mrs. Moulton swear, that Mr. Beecher explicitly confessed the adultery to them—confessed it with tears and anguish, and with passionate entreaties for forgiveness or pity. And the "Examining Committee of Plymouth Church" called Tilton to account in October, 1873—a year before the great public disclosures—for having, in August, 1870, accused Mr. Beecher of adultery, in the presence of Mrs. Bradshaw. Both Mr. Beecher and Mr. Tilton were present at a church meeting held on the 31st October, 1873. Tilton stood accused of slandering his pastor. He rose and challenged Mr. Beecher to accuse him. But Mr. Beecher, with the charge of adultery there in writing before him, made by this very man to members of Plymouth Church, preferred no complaint against his accuser. "He asks me," said Mr. Beecher, "if I have any charge to make against him. I have none. Whatever differences have been between us have been amicably adjusted, and, so far as I am concerned, buried. I have no charges." Mr. Beecher knew at this time that Tilton had accused him of adultery; but he merely declared that he had "buried" all "differences." The paper recapitulating the charges of adultery is, as Mr. Evarts stated on the trial, "in the archives of Plymouth Church."*

The direct testimony of the plaintiff and his witnesses cannot, however, be totally shut out from consideration. To take it for granted that all the witnesses on one side are perjurers would, no doubt, be an easy method of settling the case; but to accept that view without question would settle something else besides—it would practically abolish the system of trial by jury. The duty of weighing evidence would no longer be deemed necessary. The wealthy or the popular would be able to commit any offenses they pleased, and afterwards escape responsibility by saying that their accusers were perjurers. The maintenance of justice, blind to all distinctions of wealth, intellect, or position, is of much greater importance to a nation than the preservation of any individual reputation, however valuable that reputation may be. In this case, then, as in any other, the evidence on both sides must be fairly collated and examined, and the direct testimony of witnesses, where it is conflicting, must be considered in close connection with the indirect and circumstantial evidence. We must see how far the admissions, the letters, and the general conduct of the chief personages involved tend to support or refute their own personal statements. The defense trusts much to a particular set of probabilities which they place before the public. Is it likely, they ask, that a man in Mr. Beecher's position would have committed this crime? It might be deemed sufficient to ask, in answer to that, is it likely that Mr. Beecher, being innocent, would have written the letters which he did write, and would have pursued the general line of conduct, after a monstrous and unjust charge had been brought against him, which he un-

* Abbott's *Report of the Trial of Henry Ward Beecher*, I., 409.

questionably did pursue? The construction of different sets of hypotheses cannot enable us to form a judgment on an issue of this kind. It is the actual conduct of the persons involved in the case, the evidence of their own acts and admissions, which must guide us to a decision.

The counsel on the part of Mr. Beecher have treated the charge as one which originated entirely with Tilton and the Moultons. They apparently overlooked the fact that the real accusers are not Theodore Tilton and the Moultons, but Mrs. Tilton and Henry Ward Beecher. It is these two persons who have supplied the evidence which has produced the deepest impression upon the public mind.

Mrs. Tilton made the first confession of her guilt on the 3d of July, 1870. The paper signed by Mrs. Tilton on the 29th of December, 1870, was a partial repetition of her original confession, and it is alleged that this—the only "confession" acknowledged by the defendant's counsel—was extorted from Mrs. Tilton by her husband. The improbabilities which surround the coercion theory are overwhelming. As a general rule, a husband would find it no easy task to compel his wife to take any course which would bring the slightest discredit on herself or her household. But that the mother of several children, a deeply religious and pious woman (as she is represented by Mr. Beecher to be), should be coerced into writing a charge against her pastor that he had "solicited her to be a wife to him, together with all that this implied, there not being the slightest ground for such an accusation—such a story will seem to every woman in the world to be unnatural and monstrous. But, apart from theories or conjectures, it is clear that, if any undue influence was brought to bear upon Mrs. Tilton, it was when she was made to *retract* her confession. This statement we have from the woman herself, in a document which has never been challenged. It incidentally admits that the original confession was made, not in December, 1870, but in the previous July. The statement is so important that we must print it entire. It is dated December 16, 1872:

"In July, 1870, prompted by my duty, I informed my husband that H. W. Beecher, my friend and pastor, had solicited me to be a wife to him, together with all that this implied. Six months afterwards my husband felt impelled by the circumstances of a conspiracy against him, in which Mrs. Beecher had taken part, to have an interview with Mr. Beecher.

"In order that Mr. B. might know exactly what I had said to my husband, I wrote a brief statement (I have forgotten in what form), which my husband showed to Mr. Beecher. Late the same evening Mr. B. came to me (lying very sick at the time), *and filled me with distress, saying I had ruined him*—and wanting to know if I meant to appear against him. This I certainly did not mean to do, *and the thought was agonizing to me.* I then signed a paper *which he wrote,* to clear him in case of a trial. In this instance, as in most others, when absorbed by one great interest or feeling, the harmony of my mind is entirely disturbed, and I found on reflection that this paper was so drawn as to place me most unjustly against my husband, and on the side of Mr. Beecher. So, in order to repair *so cruel a blow to my long-suffering husband,* I wrote an explanation of the first paper and my signature. Mr. Moulton procured from Mr. B. the statement which I gave to him in my agitation and excitement, and now holds it

"This ends my connection with the case.

(Signed,) "ELIZABETH R. TILTON."

This remarkable statement seems, in itself, sufficient to settle three things—first, that the woman retracted her confession unwillingly, and then not because it was untrue, but because Mr. Beecher had worked upon her feelings; secondly, that Mr. Beecher taxed her with having ruined him, which it is scarcely supposable he could or would have done had he been an innocent man; thirdly, that even at this late date Mrs. Tilton regarded her husband as "long-suffering," and repented of a "cruel blow" she had dealt him. Would it have been a cruel blow to have withdrawn a wholly unjust charge against her pastor, which had been extorted from her? Or would a wife, who had been the victim of her husband's cruelties and base conspiracies, be likely to describe him as a "long suffering" man?

That the retraction which she gave to Mr. Beecher was actually *dictated* by him is proved by another highly important document. It is a letter from Mrs. Tilton to her husband, dated Dec. 30, 1870—the night of the day on which Mr. Beecher obtained the retraction of the original charge:

"MIDNIGHT.

"MY DEAR HUSBAND: I desire to leave with you before going to sleep a statement that Mr. Henry Ward Beecher called upon me this evening and asked me if I would defend him against any accusations in a council of ministers, and I replied solemnly that I would, in case the accuser was any other than my husband. *He dictated the letter, which I copied as my own,* to be used by him *against any other accuser than my husband.*

"This letter was designed to vindicate Mr. Beecher against all other persons save only my husband. I was ready to give him this letter because he said that upon that matter the letter in your hands addressed to him, dated Dec. 29, had struck him dead and ended his usefulness. You and I both are pledged to do our best to avoid publicity. God send a speedy end to all further anxieties.

"Affectionately,

"ELIZABETH."

Mrs. Tilton not only made the charge against Mr. Beecher, but she invariably adopted a tone of penitence for her own crime and sympathy for her husband when he was at a distance from home. In one of these letters she says of Mr. Beecher: "He has been the guide of our youth, and until the three last dreadful years, when our confidence was shaken in him, we trusted him as no other human being." A letter which makes a still more unmistakable reference to some terrible event in her life, known and admitted by herself and her husband, is that dated from Marietta, Ohio, November, 1870. It is impossible for any person to read it carefully without seeing that it involves an admission of her own grave misconduct in every line. She is writing to her husband:

"When, by your threats, my mother cried out in agony to me, 'Why, what have you done, Elizabeth, my child?' her worst suspicions were aroused, and I laid bare my heart then, that from my lips, and not yours, she might *receive the dagger into her heart.*"

Could such language as this apply to an ordinary domestic quarrel? Or to any transaction such as Mr. Beecher now says alone marked his intercourse with the Tiltons? What sense or meaning could there be in a woman using it who had merely been the victim of her husband's neglect or brutality? The letter goes on:

"Did not my dear child (Florence) learn enough by insinuation, that her sweet, pure soul agonized in secret, *till she broke out with the dreadful question? I know not but it hath been her death blow.*"

Are we to regard this passage as destitute of any meaning whatever? What was the dreadful question, and why should the mother's answer to it have been of such a nature as that she feared it would kill her child? She continues thus:

"When you say to my beloved brother, 'Mr. B.' preaches to forty of his mistresses every Sunday, then follow with the remark that after my death *you have a dreadful secret to reveal,* need he be told any more ere the sword pass into his soul?"

There is no pretense here that the "secret" was merely a false charge—no complaint of injustice, no defense of herself, even when she had been accused to her own mother and brother. Nor is it denied that Tilton really had a "dreadful secret" to reveal. The ground assumed is that the husband was ungenerous in disclosing the secret, not that he was guilty of falsehood, for Mrs. Tilton says that she herself elected to tell the secret to her mother; and taken in connection with the allusion to the forty mistresses, it is difficult to conjecture what she could mean except one thing. Indeed, she substantially declares her love for Mr. Beecher. She says: "Would you suffer were I to cast a shadow on any lady whom you love? Certainly, if you have any manliness you would. Even so, every word, look, or intimation *against Mr. B.*, though I be in no wise brought in, is an agony beyond the piercing of myself a hundred times." She adds a postscript for her mother, in

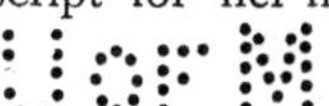

which she says: "I should mourn greatly if my life was to be made yet known to father; *his head would be bowed indeed to the grave.*" Is it possible that these are merely the expressions of a perfectly pure and innocent woman—the victim of a husband's cruelty? Again, when on July 4, 1871, Mrs. Tilton wrote a letter in which she said that she had been "misled by a good man," we see no other explanation of the passage than that she *had* been misled—though to what extent the letter itself does not say. Read in connection with the woman's other letters and "confessions," it seems scarcely possible to ascribe two meanings to it.

The charge itself, then, unquestionably originated with Mrs. Tilton, in a confession made voluntarily to her husband, and repeated, as she tells us, to her mother. Her own letters down to a certain date substantially repeat her confession over and over again.

II.—*MR. BEECHER'S RELATIONS TO THE PARTIES.*

The knowledge that such letters were in existence as those from which we have just quoted early convinced Mr. Beecher's friends that it would be indispensable to admit the existence of some peculiar or unusual intimacy between Mr. Beecher and Mrs. Tilton. It could not be pretended that they were all written under coercion, because, in every instance save one, they were written to the husband when he was at a distance from the wife. The explanation which was offered in this dilemma was that Mrs. Tilton really had been in love with Mr. Beecher, but that he never returned her affection, and was shocked when he discovered its existence.

Mr. Beecher's admissions in his evidence proved that he was on terms of extreme intimacy with Mrs. Tilton—an intimacy which cannot be usual between pastors and the female members of their congregations, or husbands would hesitate to admit ministers to their households. It rather resembles the position once taken up by the Romish priesthood towards the family, and which led to the scandals that did so much to bring about the Reformation. One incident connected with this long intimacy was related by a man who could have had no motive for seeking to injure either Mr. Beecher or Mrs. Tilton. Mr. Richards, the brother of Mrs. Tilton (who gave his evidence with manifest pain and reluctance), testified that on a certain occasion, when he visited his sister's, he was the witness of a strange scene. He thus describes it:

"I called at the house, and was in the upper story—the second story, I think. I descended to the parlor floor, and opened the door of the parlor, which was closed, and I saw Mr. Beecher seated in the front room, and Mrs. Tilton making a very hasty motion, and with a highly-flushed face, away from the position that Mr. Beecher occupied. It was such a situation as left an indelible impression on my mind."

It is hard to believe that a brother would perjure himself in order to make such a statement about an only sister.

Mr. Beecher himself tells us that, prior to the close of 1870, he had been in the habit of making the Tilton dwelling a sort of second home. "I was glad to resort to it," he said; "it was where people could not find me." He admits, too, that he brought the powerful art of flattery to bear upon Mrs. Tilton. "I spoke to her in great admiration of some letters which she showed me which she had written, one in particular, and a variety of such things; *it was entering into her life, and, in some sense, giving her an interest in my own.*" He describes in these words a relationship which a man usually reserves for his own wife, and which he can seldom transfer to another man's wife without danger. Mr. Beecher also stated in his evidence (April 13) that he was in the habit of kissing Mrs. Tilton. Whereupon Mr. Fullerton asked him, "Were you in the habit of kissing her when you went to her house in the absence of her husband?" and Mr. Beecher replied, "Sometimes I did and sometimes I did not." Again, in his letter to Plymouth

Church (July 15, 1874), he admits that there had been indiscretions on his part which caused him the "sharpest pangs of sorrow," while he denied that there was actual guilt. Those, therefore, who say that there never was anything unusual in the intimacy between Mr. Beecher and Mrs. Tilton, go far beyond Mr. Beecher himself. They set up a defense (as in other material parts of the case) which the defendant has emphatically contradicted. There was love—but it was unrequited love. In Mr. Beecher's own version of his conversation with Mrs. Moulton on the subject, given in evidence on the 12th of April, he said he had then admitted having "wrought in that good little woman a smouldering fire; that it had burned unknown to me within her, and finally it broke out with such infinite mischief." He also said (April 3) that when Moulton made the statement to him that Mrs. Tilton loved "his [Beecher's] little finger better than Theodore Tilton's whole body," "*I accepted it;* I had no means of contradicting it." Yet it must seem to the ordinary observer that an innocent man, placed in such a position, would naturally have received such a statement with infinite surprise. Mr. Beecher further admitted that Mrs. Tilton had "allowed the tendrils of her affection to grow up upon him." Whether Mrs. Tilton did indeed act in the way which is alleged on the part of Mr. Beecher—whether she immodestly forced a love upon him which he did not want, and could not return—may be doubted from the evidence, but it is the imputation which the defendant has deliberately fastened upon her. Supposing it to be well founded, it then becomes hard to understand how Mrs. Tilton can be called the stainless saint and the model of purity which Mr. Beecher himself has described her at various subsequent periods.

There were other parties to the case besides Mrs. Tilton with whom Mr. Beecher was on remarkable terms of friendship. It is true that they are now denounced as conspirators and perjurers—but not by Mr. Beecher himself, as we shall see farther on. That Mr. and Mrs. Moulton were frequently consulted by Mr. Beecher throughout these troubled years, concerning some great and difficult trouble, cannot be questioned, seeing that it rests upon evidence supplied by Mr. Beecher's own hand and from his own mouth.

In his letter to Moulton of June 1st, 1873, he wrote, "Your noble wife, too, has been to me one of God's comforters. It is such as she that renews a waning faith in womanhood." And he went on in a strain which it is difficult to make applicable to the ordinary relationships or intercourse of life:

"For a thousand encouragements—for service that no one can appreciate who has not been as sore-hearted as I have been, for your honorable delicacy, for confidence and affection—I owe you so much that I can neither express nor pay it. Not the least has been the great-hearted kindness and trust which your noble wife has shown, and which have lifted me out of despondencies often, though sometimes her clear truthfulness has laid me pretty flat."

These ardent acknowledgments of "services" to a "sore heart" accord, it must be admitted, rather with Mrs. Moulton's version of Mr. Beecher's confidences in her than with the theory of Mr. Beecher's counsel, that she is a low and degraded conspirator and perjurer. In explanation of the above letter, Mr. Beecher himself said in his evidence, "My whole intercourse with Mrs. Moulton was one which inspired in me a sense of affectionate respect and of gratitude." And again he said (April 12): "Mrs. Moulton was a lady—thoroughbred, to my apprehension; and I never heard her say a word that jarred upon my sense of the delicacy and propriety of a lady's tongue." In the same day's evidence he declared that Mrs. Moulton "was like a bank of spring flowers" to him. And yet all this time, according to the present theory of the defense, she was planning with others a deep-laid and devilish plot against his honor.

Another person with whom he was on curious terms, and whom he permitted to address him in a tone which most men would never have tolerated for a moment, was the mother of

Mrs. Tilton — Mrs. Morse. She constantly assumed the position towards him of a woman who had some strong hold and claim upon him through her knowledge of a damning secret. She wrote a letter to Mr. Beecher (dated October 24, no year, cited in evidence April 14), in which she uses this remarkable language: "Do come and see me. I will promise that the 'secret of her life,' as she calls it, shall not be mentioned. I know it's hard to bring it up, as you must have suffered intensely, and we all will, I fear, till released by death." Here, again, is an allusion to a "secret" which could not possibly have been unknown to Mr. Beecher, because Mrs. Morse says she knows he has "suffered intensely" on account of it. What was the secret thus referred to by mother and daughter? Mr. Beecher had asked Mrs. Morse to call him her son, and she writes, "When I have told darling, I felt if you could in *safety to yourself* and all concerned, you would be to me all this endearing name. Am I mistaken?" This letter was handed by Mr. Beecher to Moulton, in common with other papers bearing upon the case. "It was a dangerous letter to have around," said Mr. Beecher when he gave Moulton the letter.*

There is a still more startling letter from Mrs. Morse to Mr. Beecher, produced in evidence January 14, after a prolonged and earnest resistance on the part of defendant's counsel. It was evidently written in the first week of November, 1870, and its authenticity has never been questioned. It begins by reproaching Mr. Beecher for not having "attended to the request I [Mrs. Morse] left at your house over two weeks since," and then proceeds to berate him for not having done anything for "Elizabeth." Presently she goes on thus: "You say, keep quiet. I have all through her married life done so, and we now see our error. * * * The publicity he has given to this recent and most crushing of all trouble is what's taken the life out of her. I know of twelve persons whom he has told, and they in turn have told others." Told what? At this period—November, 1870—Mr. Beecher says

* See Abbott's *Report*, I., 439.

he had no idea that even a suspicion was entertained in reference to him and Mrs. Tilton. And yet, here is Mrs. Tilton's own mother writing to him in reference to a secret which was manifestly known to him and to her. But mark the extraordinary language which she proceeds to use: "Do you know, when I hear of you cracking your jokes from Sunday to Sunday, and think of the misery you have brought upon us, I think with the Psalmist, 'There is no God.'?" She goes on to say that, admitting it all to be the "invention of his [Tilton's] half-drunken brain, the effect is the same, for everybody believes it." She complains of him for not getting her brother into the custom-house, and says "Elizabeth was as disappointed" as herself. And then, referring to Tilton, she says: "He swears as soon as her breath leaves her body, *he will make this whole thing public*, and this prospect, I think, is one thing which keeps her living."

Now, no specific charge is made in this letter; but the whole tone of it is clearly that of a woman who knows that a man has done her daughter a great injury, and feels that she has a claim upon that man. If we ask, "Is it likely that a mother would thus assume her daughter's guilt?" we are met by another inquiry, "Is it likely that a minister of the gospel would allow a woman to address him in this threatening and insolent strain, if he did not, in some way or other, feel that he was at her mercy?" Mr. Beecher handed this letter over to Moulton. Mr. Fullerton asked him why he had done so? He answered (April 19) that Mr. Moulton was "the depositary of all the papers that related in any way, directly or indirectly, to the case." He thus admitted that the letter did relate to the case. His answer to the letter was cautious, but by no means that which any one might have supposed he would have returned to so impudent a series of demands and reproaches.

III.—*HOW THE CHARGE WAS MET.*

We have next to consider the way in which Mr. Beecher met the charge—and this is one of the vital parts of the case.

How an entirely innocent man would have acted, when unjustly accused by an intimate friend of attempting to seduce his wife, Mr. Beecher's chief counsel, Mr. Evarts, took great, and as some will think injudicious, pains to describe. He said :

> "Ah! gentlemen, we must look this crime in its face. Why, there is not a sailor in Wapping, with a strumpet on either knee, badgered and beaten in the debauches of long voyages and frequent ports, but that if a comrade should venture to suggest to him that he had seduced the daughter of an old shipmate, or the wife of a young comrade, he would bury the sheath-knife in the heart of his accuser. There has never been a coarse and vulgar debauchee voluptuary, that would flaunt his wealth and his vices in the face of our citizens here or in New-York, and ride the four-in-hand of his riches, packed with courtezans, the fact that one of his boon companions should accuse him of seducing the companion of his daughter, the wife of his friend, who had been trusted to his care, but that would send a bullet through the heart of his accuser."

That, probably, is the kind of impulse, wrong or right, which most men would feel under these trying circumstances. But when Mr. Evarts laid so much stress upon it, he imprudently forgot how different was the course which his client pursued. Mr. Beecher did not in any way resent the insult. He did not even go to any old and trusted member of his church to take counsel on the subject. He went to a comparatively slight acquaintance—Mr. Moulton. He showed no indignation over an accusation which might well have stirred the most sluggish nature. The first thing which happened after he was commanded by Tilton to resign his position and quit Brooklyn was this : he obeyed a peremptory summons to go to Moulton's house to meet Tilton on the very night of the Plymouth Church prayer-meeting. It was most inconvenient for him to go. His church expected him. But Moulton, who brought the summons, would take no denial. Mr. Beecher sent a message in hot haste requesting some one else to occupy his place at the Plymouth Church services. The prayer-meeting was neglected in order that the pastor might be led against his will to an interview with a man who had just ordered him to depart from church and home. He then manages to see Mrs. Tilton, and causes her to write the letter of retraction. This he does unknown to the husband. It is from the wife that Tilton afterwards hears that the letter had been written—not from Beecher.

What happened next is still more remarkable. We do not hear of any protest from Mr. Beecher—of any consultation with a lawyer, with Mr. Shearman, or the famous Mr. Tracy. On the very next day he parts with the letter of retraction, and on the day following that he dictated the celebrated "letter of contrition." That he did say substantially what is to-day found written in that document, no one who reads his cross-examination can for a moment doubt. Mr. Fullerton took the letter clause by clause, and asked Mr. Beecher whether he said this or that, or not? After much dexterous and elaborate fencing with the question, Mr. Beecher was in every case obliged at last to answer, "I did." We must quote one or two examples of this kind:

FIRST INSTANCE.

Mr. Fullerton—I call your attention now, Mr. Beecher, still further to this document: "He would have been a better man in my circumstances than I have been." Did you say anything to that effect?

Mr. Beecher—I did not say that sentence that I recollect, sir, but I said something which I can well understand might have been put down for short in that sentence.

Q.—Did you say anything that conveyed that sentiment? A.—*I did.*

SECOND INSTANCE.

Mr. Fullerton—I read another sentence: "I can ask nothing except that he will remember all the other hearts that would ache." Did you say anything that conveyed that idea?

Mr. Beecher—Not in that bold way.

Q.—Well, how did you say it—did you say that in substance? A.—Not in its apothegmatic form, as it stands there.

Q.—Did you express that sentiment, whether you clothed it in that language? A.—*I discoursed with him.*

Q.—Did you express that sentiment? A.—No, not in that close way in which you press me for an answer.

Q.—Well, something akin to it? A.—I can give you almost the very thing.

Q.—Something akin to it—something in that neighborhood? A.—I DID, SIR.

And so on, throughout the cross-examination.

Moreover, Mr. Beecher admits that he wrote with his own hand, at the foot of the letter, "I have trusted this to Moulton in confidence. Henry Ward Beecher." As this fact has been denied, we must once more quote from Mr. Beecher's own evidence:

Cross-examination of Mr. Beecher, April 15.

Q.—You did not then put your name to that paper for the purpose of authenticating it? A.—*I put my name to that—*

Q.—I ask you that question, and I want you to answer it. A.—I did not put my name to that paper for the purpose of authenticating the form of its contents.

Q.—You say—

"I have trusted this to Moulton in confidence."

A.—Yes.

Q.—That is your handwriting, I believe? A.—*I think it is, sir.*

Q.—Well, have you any doubt about it? A.—*No, sir; I have no doubt about it;* I think it is.

It is a great tax on ordinary credulity to be asked to believe that Mr. Beecher would have written these words on a letter, and signed his name to them, and then have handed over the letter to a third person for use, without knowing or surmising what were its contents. Moreover, in a note from Mr. Beecher to Moulton, dated June 1, 1873, he thus refers to this document: "The agreement was made after *my letter* through you was written." Here he distinctly acknowledges it as his own production, and calls it a *letter*—and he was forced to repeat that acknowledgment in his cross-examination.

And what does this letter say? "I ask, through you, Theodore Tilton's forgiveness, and I humble myself before him as I do before my God." Why? Because Tilton had accused him of seducing his wife? It is strange to find an innocent man, writhing under so outrageous a charge as that, talking of "humbling" himself before his accuser. "I will die before any one but myself shall be inculpated." Inculpated through what? It seems, then, that there were *two* persons liable to be "inculpated." This treatment of the charge is less like a denial of it than an admission. "I will only ask him to remember the other hearts that would ache." Why should a man who had been wrongfully accused of seducing a friend's wife write such a letter as this to the friend within three days of the accusation? Who was the injured man—Beecher or Tilton? Beecher, according to the theory of the defense. And yet here and everywhere else in the case we find him "humbling himself before Tilton," and pleading for mercy.

Let us now recapitulate the events of five days—five memorable days. How do Mr. Beecher's actions and conduct on those days accord with the theory of his innocence?

Monday, Dec. 26.—Tilton sends a note to Beecher demanding his retirement from Plymouth Church and Brooklyn. The following is the document—an extraordinary one for an innocent man to receive without taking instant steps to punish or expose the person who sent it:

"DEC. 26, 1870, BROOKLYN.

"HENRY WARD BEECHER—*Sir:* I demand that, for reasons which you explicitly understand, you immediately cease from the ministry of Plymouth Church, and that you quit the City of Brooklyn as a resident.

(Signed,) "THEODORE TILTON."

Thursday, Dec. 29—Mrs. Tilton writes her confession.

Friday, Dec. 30.—Mr. Beecher receives a peremptory summons to go to Moulton's house to meet Tilton. He goes. Mr. Fullerton puts this question to him: "Then you went off at the beck of the man who had insulted you on the 26th, to know what he wanted?" Mr. Beecher answered, "I did, sir." He is told of Mrs. Tilton's confession, and charged with the adultery. After leaving Moulton's house, Mr. Beecher goes to Tilton's, and induces Mrs. Tilton to retract her charge.

Saturday, Dec. 31.—Moulton goes to Beecher's house and tells him he has acted basely in forcing the retraction from Mrs. Tilton. Thereupon, Beecher hands over the retraction to Moulton.

Sunday, Jan. 1, 1871.—Beecher dictates the celebrated letter of contrition, in which he "humbles himself before Theodore Tilton as before his God," and pleads for forgiveness.

But now we are face to face with another extraordinary fact. On the 7th of February, 1871—more than a month after Tilton had accused Beecher of a crime which his counsel says would have justified him in "burying a knife" in Tilton's heart—he writes to Moulton an urgent request that he will make him and Tilton friends again. And he adds: "Theodore will have the *hardest task in such a case*, but has he not proved himself capable of the noblest things?" So that we are to understand that to accuse an intimate friend and a pastor of adultery is a "noble thing." And the wrongfully-accused man is to go to his accuser and beg his forgiveness. And the false accuser—traitor, villain, perjurer—is to be conceded to have the hardest part to play in the reconciliation. These are startling propositions to lay down—and yet they are the only deductions to be drawn from the theory of the defense. Another difficult fact to explain is that whenever Mr. Beecher wrote a letter on this subject, he always referred to Tilton as an ill-used man. Thus, in his letter denouncing Dr. Storrs, he says: "I am in hopes that Theodore, *who has borne so much*, will be unwilling to be a flail in Storrs' hand to strike at a friend." Always there is the same fear of Tilton, and the same anxiety to induce him to be silent. In his letter of February 7th, 1871, to Moulton, he says: "Of course I can never speak with her [Mrs. Tilton] again, except with his permission." Why should he assume that this condition would be imposed by the husband? He says that there was nothing wrong between himself and the wife.

On the 20th of May, 1871, Mr. Beecher, according to his own evidence (given on the 5th of April last), went to Tilton's house—not for the purpose of "burying a knife in his heart," but in order to plead again for forgiveness. He thus describes what took place—we purposely follow Mr. Beecher's own narrative:

"I only know that when I went in Mr. Tilton received me moodily, and that after a little conversation and explanation which took place he became gracious, and that he fell into an easy and unbusiness-like chat; and that in the course of it, sitting there in the old-fashioned way in his house, I went up and argued the matter—sat down on his knee in order to make the appeal closer, and when I was sitting there Mrs. Tilton came into the room and burst out laughing; I recollect the interview, and I think when she came into the room she came up and kissed me very cordially."

Thus, the victim of a charge which is enough to ruin any man, to say nothing of a great minister, never seeks to clear or defend himself—he merely "*appeals*" to his accuser, and sits down on his accuser's knee to "make the appeal closer."

We are unable to discover any time at which Mr. Beecher attempted to defend himself until the charge against him had been made public through the newspapers. Then something had to be said and done. From the 30th December, 1870, down to last summer, he was incessantly engaged in a despairing effort to conceal something which, if made known, he felt sure would ruin him. The Moultons evidently knew the secret; and his piteous appeals to Mr. Moulton to help him are on record in his own letters. In all this correspondence, Mr. Beecher constantly represented himself as the offender. Down to so late a period as June 1, 1873, Mr. Beecher wrote to Moulton a letter in which his own culpability and Tilton's past generosity are assumed as perfectly well understood between all the parties. He says in the course of the letter: "He [Tilton] had condoned his wife's fault." Very strange language, considering that the wife had committed *no* fault. Of course this fatal passage could not be reconciled with the general theory of the defense—that Mr. Beecher and Mrs. Tilton were both ill-used persons, and perfectly innocent of all wrong. Consequently, Mr. Evarts suggested that the "fault" in Mrs. Tilton above referred to was that of having divided her affections between her husband and Mr. Beecher. But in a previous part of his speech Mr. Evarts declared that she had never acted thus—that Mr. Beecher had been "imposed upon" when he was led to believe that she had. One of the most curious features of the defense is the rapidity with which Mr. Beecher's legal advisers have from time to time substituted one theory for another—constructing elaborate chains of explanations, then repudiating them, then returning to them, then discarding them again, and so on *ad infinitum*. Every theory which Mr. Beecher put forward to account for his conduct *before* the trial was expressly contradicted by himself or his counsel *upon* the trial. Every theory advanced by Mr. Beecher during the trial is expressly contradicted by his own former admissions and letters.

Mr. Beecher knew, after the 30th December, 1870, that he was accused of adultery. He must have known, months before, that Tilton accused him of it; but it was not until December that he found out that the charge *rested on Mrs. Tilton's own confession*. The letters, conversations, and negotiations which from that time forth passed between all the chief personages in this miserable tragedy obviously proceeded upon the understanding that Mr. Beecher had committed some grave offense, the consequences of which would be utter destruction to him, so that rather than face them he cried out for death. That was the common ground on which all these persons met. It is the key, and apparently the only key, to the long series of letters, compromises, and interviews. The fact of guilt was taken for granted on all sides. It was acknowledged in all Mr. Beecher's interviews with Moulton and Mrs. Moulton, it had been confessed to Mrs. Tilton's mother by *herself* (as the Marietta letter conclusively shows), and it was proclaimed by Mr. Beecher in all his letters. On the 7th of February, 1871, he implores Mrs. Tilton to trust implicitly to Mr. Moulton's guidance. "His hand it was," he says, "that tied up the storm that was ready to burst upon our heads." What necessity was there for using language of this sort to a woman who had done no wrong, and could have no reason to fear any storm? In February, 1872—exactly a year later—Mr. Beecher offers * to abandon his church and position altogether if Tilton felt disposed to exact such a penalty. "If my destruction," he wrote, "would place him, Theodore, all right, that shall not stand in the way. I am willing to step down and out. * * * I do not think that anything would be gained by it. I should be destroyed, but he would not be saved. E. and the children would have their future clouded." The last sentence is full of dreadful meaning. It is a plain admission that something had taken place which, if known, would not only ruin Mr. Beecher, but *cloud the future* even of Tilton's children. What was there to *destroy* Mr. Beecher in his having advised Bowen to discharge Tilton, or suggesting a separation between man and wife—even if he had done these things? Or how many acts can a mother commit which will "cloud the future" of her children? The same kind of reference to the children appears in Mr. Beecher's letter to Moulton of June 1, 1873. Referring to Tilton, he says: "He had enjoined upon me with the utmost earnestness and solemnity *not to betray his wife, nor leave his children to a blight.* I had honestly and earnestly joined in

* See letter to Moulton, pp. 382-4 of Abbott's *Report.*

the purpose."* Supposing Mr. Beecher to be innocent, how *could* he have betrayed Tilton's wife? What was there to reveal? The language which he declares that Tilton used to him exactly coincides with the position described by the wit nesses—namely that the adultery was admitted, but that Tilton wished to keep the fact a secret for the sake of his wife and children, and did so keep it until he was accused of conspiracy by Plymouth Church. Mr. Beecher went on in the same letter to declare that he was suffering "the torments of the damned," and that he was living "on the sharp and ragged edge of anxiety, remorse, fear, despair." Why remorse? And above all, why *fear?* Supposing that he advised the wife to leave her husband—which is purely a supposition—why fear *for himself?* He protests that he had done all he could "to allay prejudices against Tilton," and to suppress "tendencies which, if not stopped, *would break out into* ruinous defense of me." How could the defense of Tilton ruin Beecher? And why should Mr. Beecher have been so anxious to keep all his friends from defending him, unless from the fear of provoking Tilton to make public explanations—the very catastrophe which afterwards happened?

Even when Tilton reproached Beecher for forcing Mrs. Tilton to retract her charge, what was the minister's attitude? Did he turn upon his accuser in indignation? No—he simply complained that he thought "an unfair advantage had been taken of him." Tilton rejoined that it was he who had acted unfairly, in extorting the retraction. "*I argued the point with him,*" says Mr. Beecher. (Evidence, April 15.) It is difficult to imagine a man, who had been innocently accused of adultery, condescending to argue such a "point" with the scoundrel who had trumped up the charge Mr. Beecher had obtained a retraction to which, on his own version of the affair, he was thoroughly entitled. He then apologized for having obtained it, and *handed it back to Moulton.* The ordinary principles or motives upon which human conduct can be ex-

* See Abbott's *Report*, I., 402.

plained utterly fail to reconcile such a course as this with conscious innocence.

It is impossible to feel surprise that all the ingenuity of Mr. Beecher's counsel failed to convince the jury, and has failed to convince the public, that Mr. Beecher's method of meeting this charge was worthy of a Christian minister, or could have been prompted by a "conscience void of offense." Mr. Beecher has told a dozen different stories in explanation of his letters and conduct—and every one of them crushes the other. Apart, moreover, from the versions of the affair given by the witnesses on the trial, there are the letters of the principal persons in the case; and the endless efforts which have been made to place an innocent construction upon these letters fail to reduce them to a level with ordinary correspondence. The following quotations clearly relate to the same transaction, whatever that may have been, and they demand the most careful attention. We bring them together here for the purpose of comparison:

MRS. TILTON TO HER HUSBAND.

"Oh, my dear husband, may you never need the discipline of being misled by a good woman as I have been by a good man."

"When, by your threats, my mother cried out in agony to me, 'Why, what have you done, Elizabeth, my child?' her worst suspicions were aroused, and I laid bare my heart then, that from my lips, and not yours, she might *receive the dagger into her heart.*"

"Did not my dear child, Florence, learn enough by insinuation, that her sweet, pure soul agonized in secret, *till she broke out with the dreadful question?* I know not but it hath been her death-blow."

"When you say to my beloved brother, 'Mr. B.' preaches to forty of his mistresses every Sunday, then follow with the remark that after my death *you have a dreadful secret to reveal*, need he be told any more ere the sword pass into his soul!"

"Would you suffer were I to cast a shadow on any lady whom you love? Certainly, if you have any manliness you would. Even so, every word, look, or intimation *against Mr. B.*, though I be in no wise brought in, is an agony beyond the piercing of myself a hundred times."

(To her mother.) "I should mourn greatly if my life was to be made yet known to my father; *his head would be bowed indeed to the grave.*"

BEECHER TO MOULTON.

"I ask, through you, Theodore Tilton's forgiveness, and I humble myself before him as I do before my God."

"He [Tilton] had condoned his wife s fault. He had enjoined upon me with the utmost earnestness and solemnity *not to betray his wife, nor leave his children to a blight.*"*

"If my destruction would place him all right, that shall not stand in the way. I am willing to step down and out. I do not think that anything would be gained by it. *I should be destroyed*, but he would not be saved. *E. and the children would have their future clouded.*"

"To live on the sharp and ragged edge of anxiety, remorse, fear, despair, and yet to put on all the appearance of serenity and happiness, cannot be endured much longer."

"Would to God, who orders all hearts, that by your kind mediation, Theodore, Elizabeth, and I could be made friends again. Theodore will have the hardest task in such a case; but has he not proved himself capable of the noblest things? I wonder if Elizabeth knows how generously he has carried himself towards me."†

MRS. MORSE TO MR. BEECHER.

"Do come and see me. I will promise *that the secret of her life*, as she calls it, shall not be mentioned. I know it's hard to bring it up, as you must have suffered intensely, and we all will, I fear, till released by death."

"The publicity he [Tilton] has given to this recent and most crushing of all trouble is what's taken the life out of her. I know of twelve persons whom he has told, and they in turn have told others."

"Do you know, when I hear of you cracking your jokes from Sunday to Sunday, and think of the misery you have brought upon us, I think with the Psalmist, 'There is no God.'"

* See Abbott's *Report*, I., 02. † Abbott's *Report* I., 373-74.

"He [Tilton] swears, as soon as her breath leaves her body he will *makc this whole thing public*, and this prospect, I think, is one thing which keeps her living."

It cannot be pretended that these extraordinary letters are without meaning. Then what do they mean? To what "secret" do these three persons, writing to or of each other, thus constantly refer in a spirit of alarm or remorse? Can it be supposed that they were merely pursuing shadows?

IV.—*THE ANSWERS TO THE CHARGE.*

These are so few, when sifted out from the enormous mass of verbiage under which they have been buried by the lawyers, that they can be brought into a comparatively brief compass. The direct replies to the charge are all comprised in the follow ing abstract:

1. *That no accusation of adultery was ever made.* This, as we have shown, is disproved not only by the evidence of Mr. Tilton and Mr. and Mrs. Moulton, but by the letters of the two persons chiefly involved. There is nothing to support this part of the defense but the oath on the trial of the defendant himself, and with that oath his own previous course of conduct and his correspondence are disastrously in conflict.

2. *That the charge was concocted for blackmailing purposes.* Mr. Beecher has disposed of this. He only paid over, from first to last, $7,000 towards business projects in which Tilton was engaged. So far from exacting money from Mr. Beecher, Tilton, on one occasion at least, expressly refused to receive "any pecuniary or other favor" at his hands. (Tilton to Beecher, May 2, 1874). As for the $7,000, Mr. Beecher swore on the trial that he had paid it willingly. "Not the slightest pressure" was brought to bear upon him. (Beecher's evidence, April 20.) The reader had better examine Mr. Beecher's own words on this subject:

From Mr. Beecher's Cross-examination, April 20.

"Q.—Well, did you think that was obtained from you by

Mr. Moulton in any improper way? A. No; that was not my feeling at all.

Q.—You did not regard it as blackmail, then? A. I did not.

Q.—Can you tell how much was paid prior to the payment of the $5,000? A. Not accurately, sir; I have an impression that the whole sum amounted to $7,000—over that than under.

Q.—That is including the $5,000? A. Including the $5,000.

Q.—Was the $2,000 paid before the payment of the $5,000? A. Yes, sir, I think so.

Q.—Did you pay any after the $5,000? A. I think not.

Q.—Did you look at any of these payments in the light of blackmail? A. I did not, sir.

Q.—You felt entirely satisfied with the money you had given? A. And I rejoiced to be able to give.

Q.—And did it willingly? A. I did it cheerfully.

Q.—And rejoicingly? A. And rejoicingly.

Q.—Without finding any fault with anybody? A. Without finding the slightest fault.

Q.—Or thinking that you had been taken advantage of? A. I did not dream of it.

Q.—Or imposed upon? A. Or imposed upon."

In fact, Mr. Beecher admitted that the idea of blackmailing never entered his head until it was put there by those two "smart" lawyers, Tracy and Shearman. Mr. Beecher said it had been "rubbed into him" by these worthy men. Not until October, 1874, did he "give in to them"—that is, not until the Tilton and Moulton charges and papers had been published, and it was necessary to make a reply to them. It was in that desperate situation, when concealment was all over, and when something must be said to destroy the effect of Tilton's and Moulton's statements, that the blackmailing explanation was first produced. On this point Mr. Beecher's admissions are clear, and they appear to be absolutely destructive of the blackmailing hypothesis. He was asked when he finally surrendered to the Shearman-Tracy tactics:

"A.—Well, I think it was since I returned from the White Mountains.

Q.—Well, when was that? A. That was about October, 1874.

Q.—Then you gave up and came to the conclusion that it was blackmail because they told you so? A. Well, I *didn't dare to say in their presence any more that it was not blackmail; I had been so constantly disciplined by them that I did not dare to say it was not blackmail.*

Q.—Then they intimidated you and treated you a great deal worse than Moulton did? A. Oh, a great deal worse.

Q.—Mr. Beecher, your answer to the question I put to you, whether you now believe that Francis D. Moulton intended to levy blackmail upon you, has not been answered satisfactorily to some of my associates, and I will put it to you again, as to your present belief? A. Well, sir, if you mean by blackmail he levied contributions for his own advantage on me, I don't think he did.

Q.—Yes? A. But if you mean that he levied money upon me, using my generous feelings as the instrument, for the benefit of Mr. Tilton, I think he did.

Q.—Well, when did he take the advantage of using your generous feelings? A. Well, I think he did in regard to the $5,000, though I did not at the time, *and though it is entirely an after judgment and an artificial judgment.*

Q.—Entirely voluntary that payment was? A. *It was, so far as I was concerned, perfectly so.*"

And again:

"Q.—It never occurred to you, then, that the payment of this money, which gave you so much joy in it, was blackmail until you had a lawyer tell you of it? A. I was fought with and actually beaten into the use of the term. I defended Mr. Moulton up and down, and said he had no thought of the kind. I would not believe it of him, and it was in subsequent conferences that they made me. I was made ashamed of my simplicity—that is, they told me I was green."

In most cases of blackmail, it is generally the blackmailed person who first finds out, by bitter experience, that he has been victimized, and then he goes to the lawyers to get advice as to some means of saving himself. In this case the money was paid "with joy," and it required two lawyers to discover that it was really a blackmailing operation.

3. *That the charge was the result of a conspiracy.* But there must be an *animus* shown before such a theory can be established, and no successful, or even serious, attempt of the kind has been made. Mr. and Mrs. Moulton had no motive for desiring to injure Mr. Beecher. On the contrary, it is clear that they did their best for three or four years to hush the matter up, and Moulton does not hesitate to avow that he "told lies" to shield Beecher during that period, as perhaps most men would have done to save a friend under similar circumstances. The Moultons refused to stand by Mr. Beecher when he denied his own words to them, and then for the first time they were accused of being conspirators. The reward they have met with for endeavoring to shield Mr. Beecher will probably discourage them from attempting anything of that kind in future. We have also to bear in mind the fact that Mr. Beecher's and Mrs. Tilton's own letters supply most damaging evidence against them; and we thus are forced to the conclusion that if there was a conspiracy, Mr. Beecher and Mrs. Tilton must be regarded as the chief conspirators.

4. *That Tilton makes the charge from malice, and knowing it to be false.* Here, as throughout the case, it is the evidence of Mr. Beecher which overwhelms the defense set up by Mr. Beecher's lawyers. For he admits that it was Mrs. Tilton who made the charge. When he went to her room on the 20th of December, the following scene took place—described by himself in his recent evidence:

"Elizabeth, he says that you have told him that I had won your affections from him and that you had transferred the wifely affection to me," and that I think it was, though I will not be certain about that matter; the tears ran down her cheeks and she made still no response. I went on and said to her, "Elizabeth, Mr. Tilton says that you have declared to him that I have made improper advances towards you," and she was very much agitated; I said, "Elizabeth, have you ever said that to your husband?" *and she bowed her head*, and then it was that I spoke to her with more emphasis than I had done."

In his cross-examination by Mr. Fullerton, April 15, he

was asked why he did not resent the injury which Mr. Tilton had done to him in making the charge. He answered, "If the charge was a correct one he did not injure me." Surely a most remarkable answer. Presently he said, "My conclusion was that Mr. Tilton had reason for making that charge; that he *had evidence of it from his wife.*" Again—we quote question and answer: "Q.—Then you suppose Mr. Tilton was acting in good faith in making these charges against you? A. I supposed he had reason to think that I had been a wronger of his family."

One more quotation from evidence which Mr. Beecher's own counsel ought to have read before they persisted in this line of defense:

"Q.—Did you regard it simply as a charge made by Mrs. Tilton? A. Certainly I did.

Q.—And not as a charge by Theodore Tilton? A. As a charge that he represented he made from her.

Q.—Did you not understand him as making that charge on his own behalf against you? A. I had no doubt that he supposed the charge to be as she had written it to him at that time."

It is clear from these admissions of Mr. Beecher himself that he never believed either that Tilton had concocted the charge, or that Mrs. Tilton made it under coercion. In short, he upsets all the ingenious theories put forward by his own lawyers.

5. The fifth answer is that *Mrs. Tilton never confessed adultery*. Several witnesses swear that she did. Her own letters are not reasonably open to any other interpretation. It is true that she does not use the word "adultery," but her language can only relate to a great crime. And the defendant did not venture to call her, although the plaintiff offered in court to consent to her being called. Presumably she was a hostile witness to the plaintiff, and had he called her he could not have cross-examined her, and of course the other side would have had no motive for doing so. Therefore, when the plaintiff offered to interpose no objection to receiving her as a witness, he did all that he could do.

6. *Mr. Beecher swears he is innocent.* This must, of course, be taken into consideration with the fact that several witnesses swear that he repeatedly confessed his guilt to them, and that his letters go to substantiate their assertion, while on any other hypothesis it is impossible to explain them. In all such situations, it cannot be assumed that one person alone tells the truth, unless he is borne out by a powerful sequence of circumstantial evidence and his own general conduct. It is clear that Mr. Beecher is not so sustained. He had abundant opportunities for denying the charge long before the publication of 1874, but he avoided them all. One such opportunity demands special attention, since it was clearly Mr. Beecher's duty, supposing his innocence, to have instantly profited by it. A certain Mrs. Bradshaw had been a member of Plymouth Church for upwards of twenty years, was devoted to the pastor, and could not bear to hear stories repeated to his discredit. In August, 1870, as appears from the "West charges," Theodore Tilton accused Mr. Beecher of adultery, in her presence. In October 1873, the charges having by that time become more and more widely circulated, this lady wrote to Mr. Beecher asking him whether she "must accept *Theodore's awful story* for the truth." Surely Mr. Beecher ought to have said *No*, if he had been innocent. But he did not say it. He merely advised Mrs. Bradshaw [letter of October 7, 1873] not to interfere, and added "whatever differences have arisen have been amicably adjusted by those most deeply concerned." Now, here was a distinct appeal to him, made by a valued member of his congregation, to deny "Theodore's awful story" —and he refused to do it. The witnesses for the plaintiff were substantially unshaken during cross-examination, and all the documents in the case go to the verification of their narratives. There is some doubt about a date in Mrs. Moulton's evidence, but Mr. Beecher admits that he had a long interview with her somewhere about the time alleged, and the actual date is, therefore, of no importance.

7. That Mr. Beecher's remorse arose from his having

caused Tilton's dismissal by Bowen. But Bowen swears that this advice did *not* cause the dismissal in question—and the letters in the case evidently refer to some transaction of a totally different kind. Moreover, Tilton was not dismissed by Bowen until after he had made the charge against Beecher. This is proved from the records of Plymouth Church itself. The "West" charges against Tilton, for accusing Mr. Beecher of adultery, alleged that he had thus accused his pastor, in the presence of Mrs. Bradshaw, on the *3d of August*, 1870. Now Bowen did not break his contract with Tilton until December 31st, 1870. Obviously, then, the charge could not possibly have been prompted by motives of revenge for the dismissal in question.

8. *That Mr. Beecher merely advised the separation of the Tiltons.* It is sufficient to say in answer to this that no reference to the fact appears in any of his letters or conversations. All that he wrote or said manifestly referred to something of a much more serious and ruinous character. But it must also be stated that Mrs. Tilton herself denies ever having even contemplated separation from her husband. "I indignantly deny," she says (letter of January 4, 1871), that I ever sought separation from my husband." This is one of the numerous letters which Mr. Beecher's counsel found it more convenient to overlook than to explain.

Such appear to us to be the facts in this melancholy case. That they tell heavily against Mr. Beecher will be universally regretted, for it is a mournful sight to see a great preacher of religion resting even under the suspicion of a dark crime. And for the persons on the other side, it is impossible to feel pity or respect. That Tilton should have known of his wife's guilt; that he should have gone on living with her; that he should even have consulted with her alleged seducer as to the paternity of one of her children, and that, finally, he should declare on this very trial that she is a "pure, white-souled woman"—all this puts him a long way outside of the range of public sympathy. As for the woman who has been the immediate cause of these darkened homes and blighted reputations, she may be dismissed to the general contempt of mankind. A city-full of such women would not be worth the trouble and misery which this one has occasioned. She constructed a form of religion to suit her own circumstances and desires, and easily convinced herself that there was nothing wrong in her breaking her marriage vows, and afterward "sacrificing" her husband. She told her husband that Mr. Beecher knew better than he or she did what was wrong or right. Mr. Beach seems to have accurately described her ideas on the subject when he says that she held the belief that she, her husband, and Mr. Beecher might form a sort of triple "friendship," and "indulge all their desires without any infringement of the law of God or the law of morality." She calls it herself a "trinity of friendship." Revolting as such an idea must be to every decent mind, the evidence and letters afford a strong presumption that it was for years entertained by this degraded and worthless woman.

There is only one good result which can possibly follow from this exposure and trial. It may lead people in Brooklyn and elsewhere to distrust the new Gospel of Love, and to allow no priests or ministers to come between husband and wife, or to interfere with family ties or sully family honor. Lastly, it may induce them to return to the older and safer moorings which alone can prevent society from drifting into chaos. If this should be the fruit of the trial, a scandal which poisoned the air for six long months will not have been dragged to the light in vain.

www.ingramcontent.com/pod-product-compliance
Lightning Source LLC
LaVergne TN
LVHW011127110826
845150LV00008B/2265

* 9 7 8 1 4 1 8 1 9 5 0 3 8 *